Taking the l

TO THE GREAT AMERICAN SOUTHWEST

Taking the Kids
TO THE GREAT AMERICAN SOUTHWEST

Everything That's Fun to Do and See for Kids—and Parents Too!

Eileen Ogintz

HarperCollinsWest
A Division of HarperCollinsPublishers

For information address HarperCollins Publishers, 10 East 53rd Street, New York, NY 10022.

Taking the Kids is a trademark of Eileen Ogintz.

FIRST EDITION

Library of Congress Cataloging–in–Publication Data

Ogintz, Eileen.
    The Great American Southwest: everything that's fun to do and see for kids — and parents too! / Eileen Ogintz
    p. cm. — (Taking the kids)
    ISBN 0-06-258534-7 : $9.95
    1. Southwest New — Guidebooks — Juvenile literature. 2. Children-Travel — Southwest, New — Guidebooks — Juvenile literature. I. Title II. Series.
F787.035 1994   94-5457
917.904′33—dc20   CIP
                                                                            AC

94 95 96 97 98 XXX   10 9 8 7 6 5 4 3 2 1

To Matt, Reggie and Melanie, my favorite travelers;

To Andy, who helped every step of the way; and

To Grandma Minna who kept the home fires burning.

Thanks to the staffs at the Heard Museum, the Museum of Northern Arizona, the Indian Pueblo Cultural Center and the Albuquerque Museum who gladly shared their time and expertise. Thanks also to the staffs and rangers at the national parks and monuments across the Southwest; they were never too busy to answer another question. And to old friends Mark and Margaret Noblin of New Mexico's Southwest Adventure Group, for their knowledge and hospitality.

Contents

THE GRAND CANYON............................Page 9
ONE OF THE WORLD'S BIGGEST HOLES IN THE GROUND

ARIZONA INDIAN COUNTRY ....Page 19
KACHINA DOLLS, PETRIFIED LOGS AND WEAVERS

LAS VEGAS ....Page 29
THE PLACE THAT NEVER SLEEPS

JEROME, SEDONA AND BISBEE ....Page 37
MINES AND GHOSTLY PLACES

TUCSON AND PHOENIX.........................Page 43
CACTUS, COWBOYS AND FLY BALLS

WHITE SANDS NATIONAL MONUMENT ..Page 53
SAND SURFERS

CARLSBAD CAVERNS ....Page 61
STALACTITES, STALAGMITES AND THOUSANDS OF BATS

ALBUQUERQUE....................................Page 68
CHILES, CONQUISTADORS AND HOT AIR BALLOONS

NEW MEXICO PUEBLOS ....Page 77
STORIES, DANCES AND POTS

SANTA FE AND TAOS ....Page 85
FIESTAS, MUSEUMS AND ART

THE GRAND CANYON
ONE OF THE WORLD'S BIGGEST HOLES IN THE GROUND

It's one of the biggest holes in the ground you'll ever see. The Grand Canyon is more than one mile deep and 280 miles long. It's sliced through layers of solid rock and is more than 10 miles wide in some spots. Next time you're digging at the beach or in your back-yard, imagine digging a hole that big. That's even longer than a highway stretching from New York past Washington, D.C.

Nobody dug the Grand Canyon, of course. Water created it—the running water of the Colorado River as well as rain and snow. That's what makes it so amazing. It took six million years, though there are rocks at the bottom that are much older. The different colors—red and pink and yellow—come from traces of minerals in different layers of the rock—eight layers in all.

When you look at the Grand Canyon, you're seeing one of the best examples of the power of running water—of erosion—in the entire world. There's nothing like it anywhere. That's why millions of people like you and your family come to see it every year.

The Havaasupai

The only people living in the Grand Canyon today are the Havaasupai Indians. No roads go to their tiny village. You must hike down eight miles to get there. A few miles further is Havasu Canyon that includes three wonderful high waterfalls. It's a great place for swimming too.

FACT:

The earliest tourists had to come by mule, horse or wagon.

Most people visit the South Rim. There are more hotels and more scenic trails here and it is open all year.

A bird—or a plane—could quickly fly the 10 miles from the South Rim to the North Rim. But it's 220 miles by car. It is cooler and quieter, though usually open only from mid–May to mid–November.

The Inner Canyon can be reached only by foot, mule or by way of the Colorado River—on a raft, for example.

Wherever you are, there's more to do than you'll have time for—no matter how long you stay.

Stop by the Yavapai Observation Station to learn how the Canyon was formed.

Visit the Tusayan Ruins and Museum to get an idea of what life was like for the Anasazi, the Native Americans who were the Canyon's first settlers more than 800 years ago.

Think about what life must have been like for the Anasazi children.

Hiking Smarts

- Always remember to take a first aid kit.
- Bring plenty of water—a quart for every 2 miles you plan to hike. And don't forget to drink before you feel thirsty.
- Stick a few snacks like granola bars or an apple in your backpack. You can't buy anything on the trail.
- Wear comfortable shoes—not new ones—and heavy socks.
- Bring a light jacket in summer. Don't forget gloves when it's cold outside.
- Don't forget a hat (with a brim), sunglasses and plenty of sunscreen.
- Keep your trail map handy and don't hike alone. Remember, it will likely take you twice as long to get back up to the rim as it took to hike down. Allow yourself plenty of time.
- Carry a little bag for litter.
- Stay on the trails.

They lived on both rims and at the bottom of the Canyon in pueblos built out of rock. Over 2,000 Anasazi pueblo ruins have been discovered here. With their parents, they grew crops, made pottery, wove fine baskets, hunted and fished.

Walk along the rim and look out at the views. Look hard at the rock and see how many different shapes you can find. The trail along the South Rim winds for nine miles and is a great spot for taking pictures.

You can also hike down into the Canyon. Remember, hiking here is backward: you hike downhill first and then climb back up. On the South Rim, The Bright Angel Trail is popular with families. You can hike just one and a half miles down to the first resthouse or 12.2 miles to Plateau Point.

It's hard work! You can't even hike all the way down and back in one day. Hikers may stay at the rustic Phantom Ranch Lodge at the bottom or camp with reservations. You need to make arrangements far in advance of your trip.

FACT.

The Grand Canyon is as deep as some mountains are tall.

To help you explore and have fun, there are mule trips down through the Canyon to the Colorado River (you must be at least 4-feet,7-inches tall to participate). There are also raft trips—day-long smooth-water trips and week-long trips that take you over wild rapids.

Everywhere you turn, you'll see wildlife. There are hundreds of different animals here—300 kinds of birds alone. Look for the big ravens and listen to their call. Watch for monarch butterflies.

You'll see mule deer and snakes, bighorn sheep and lizards, beavers and bats, squirrels and frogs. But remember, don't feed the animals. It's bad for them.

There are lots of different kinds of wildflowers and trees

too—different types as you descend into the Canyon. Watch for the crimson monkeyflower and the prickly barrel cactus. Keep track of all of the different animals and flowers you see.

You can search for fossils or the crude drawings called petroglyphs on the Canyon walls. The Anasazi used the walls as blackboards to tell stories.

Before you start exploring, make sure to stop at the Grand Canyon National Park Visitor Center. The rangers will be glad to help you plan your visit. They also offer many programs especially for kids and their parents: fossil walks and games to teach you about rocks, campfires and talks about wildlife. The programs change weekly but parents will be glad to know they're all free.

You can also sign up to become a Junior Ranger; complete a

The Stick Mystery

They're made of single willow sticks twisted into crude shapes of animals—deer and antelope and sheep. They're thousands of years old and have been found in caves that are high in the Grand Canyon. Experts think the ancient people might have thought these little figures would bring them good luck. No one knows exactly who these people were—or why they left the figures where they did.

certain number of activities—including picking up litter—and you will qualify for a special Junior Ranger patch. You'll probably meet other kids along the way.

There's so much activity at the Grand Canyon that it's hard to believe it was largely unexplored until 1869. One Army lieutenant, in fact, had declared the area "valueless" after his trip. Earlier, Spanish explorers were frustrated when they found themselves in the Grand Canyon—and couldn't figure out how to cross the Colorado River!

We can thank John Wesley Powell, a one-armed Civil War veteran, for opening the Grand Canyon for us. Powell led the first successful trip down the Colorado River through the Canyon. He named it the Grand Canyon. Imagine if you were one of Powell's 10 men in their four small wooden boats. It took them three months to travel down the Colorado, braving the uncharted rapids. Would you have been scared? Miners followed looking for gold. Tourists weren't far behind, especially after the railroad arrived at the Canyon's South Rim in 1901. You can imagine what it must have felt like to be one of those early tourists if you take a ride on the old turn-of-the-century Grand Canyon Railway from the town of Williams to the South Rim.

There will be more activity here than ever starting in 1994: it's the Grand Canyon's 75th birthday as a national park. All that time kids and parents—millions a year—have been coming to see it. They've walked the same trails and stared down inside. The people have changed. The Canyon hasn't.

KIDS! TELL YOUR PARENTS:

The Grand Canyon is an awesome sight but visiting it is not the same as getting thrills in an amusement park. You need to be careful. There are steep drop-offs from the rim. Keep a close eye on each other.

Make sure you've got plenty of water and snacks if you're hiking.

And remember, the weather can be extreme here—100 degrees in the summer, below freezing in the winter. Be prepared with proper clothes. And don't over do it.

Carry a first aid kit, a compass and a whistle—to attract help in case of an emergency. Call 602-638-7888 for visitor information.

ARIZONA INDIAN COUNTRY
KACHINA DOLLS, PETRIFIED LOGS AND WEAVERS

The first Hopi people climbed up from the world of the spirits through a hole deep in the Grand Canyon called Sipapu, their storytellers will tell you.

Hopi have lived in Northern Arizona for nearly 1,000 years—long before Christopher Columbus discovered America. At first, their ancestors lived in caves, then pit houses and then apartment-like houses of small rooms they built out of rocks all along steep cliffs. You can still see the ruins of ancient homes at places like Walnut Canyon and Wupatki National Monument near Flagstaff, farther away at the Navajo National Monument near Tuba City and over the border in Colorado at Mesa Verde National Park, among other places. It's fun to hike around the crumbling walls, thinking about what life must have been like for children then.

One good place in Arizona to learn about Native Americans and their ancestors is the Heard Museum in Phoenix. Don't miss the hands-on "Old Ways, New Ways" area where you and your parents can do everything from walk through a Pueblo home to design a rug to beat a drum.

Another fun learning place is the Museum of Northern Arizona in Flagstaff. You can learn about the rocks and animals of Indian Country—even about the dinosaurs that once lived here. Check out the Kiva Room where you can see the inside of the traditional underground rooms where Hopi men meet and hold traditional ceremonies. These ceremonies represent the Hopis' emergence from the Underworld.

Hopi-tu means "good peaceful people" and they have always

Stargazing

Pluto was discovered by astronomers at the Lowell Observatory in Flagstaff. That was in 1930 and today astronomers here continue to study the planets and the stars. On some Friday evenings, visitors can peer through the two-foot-long Clark Telescope to see the stars themselves.

FACT:

A prehistoric 20-foot-long Dilophosaurus left tracks — three-toed footprints twice the size of a grown-up hand — down a dirt road not far from Tuba City, scientists believe.

been farmers, settling high atop three flat mesas where they hoped to be safe from their enemies. Some of their villages were built many hundreds of years ago and still don't have running water or electricity. Oraibi may be the oldest village in North America that has been lived in continuously—since more than 500 years before the Pilgrims landed at Plymouth.

FACT:

There is only one spot in the country where you can be in four states at the same time —New Mexico, Arizona, Colorado and Utah. The spot is called the "Four Corners."

If you were growing up in a Hopi village, you'd go to school, of course, but you'd also learn the ancient language and traditions. You'd be a member of your mother's clan—the Bear clan, for example, or Medicine Bowl clan. Each clan has traditional roles to play in ceremonies and in the village. As do your relatives, Hopi clan members help their children to grow up strong and well-behaved, teaching them the special traditions of their clan.

Corn, clouds and rain all have special importance to Hopis because they have always been farmers. New Hopi babies are each given an ear of white corn. And many ceremonies revolve around praying for rain and good crops. On special occasions, you might eat *piki*, a crispy bread made from blue corn.

Boys may learn traditions in the *kivas*. If you visit a Hopi village, you'll see a ladder sticking out of the kiva. But don't go down. Outsiders aren't permitted.

You'll also see *kachina* dolls everywhere. Hopi girls are given these little figures—many of them scary-looking—from the time they are little. Tourists often buy them as souvenirs but they are very important to the Hopi religion. They represent the powerful ancestor spirits who help bring rain, grow crops or make a sick person well. There are hundreds of them like QoQlo who brings a promise of good crops and toys for the children. Many dances involving kachinas are considered so special and private that they are closed to outsiders.

The Hopi also are known for their beautiful crafts like basket-

Passing By

The early Navajos believed that petrified logs were the bones of a giant monster named Yietso whom their ancestors killed when they first came here.

Today, we have a different explanation for the strange and beautiful logs at the Petrified Forest National Park, which has the largest concentration of petrified wood in the world, including one log that weighs 44 tons and is 35 feet long. Millions of years ago, tall trees fell here and were washed into a swamp. They sank to the bottom and were covered by silt and clay and volcanic ash from volcanos that were erupting then in the Southwest. Gradually, the logs, turned into the beautifully patterned, deeply colored stone you can see here—blue, yellow orange, rust and red—along the Giant Logs trail and elsewhere in the park. You can also see the land that's called the Painted Desert because of its purple, orange and pink colors. But don't take any rocks. You need to leave them for other kids to see.

If you want to see what one giant rock weighing millions of tons—a meteorite traveling more than 43,000 miles per hour—did to the Earth, head to Meteor Crater just east of Flagstaff. Stare into a giant hole 570 feet deep—a 600-story building would fit inside. It stretches more than 4,100 feet across. At least 20 football games could be played simultaneously on the crater floor. You can hike around the rocky rim—more than three miles.

The eerie terrain in Meteor Crater so closely resembles that of the moon that NASA astronauts trained here for their Apollo missions.

making, pottery and silver-making—as are their neighbors the Dine', the name the Navajo people have given themselves. It means "the people."

They're especially known for their beautiful Navajo rugs. Each rug is different and may take a Navajo woman months to make working at her big loom. That's why they're so expensive and admired.

The Dine' haven't been here quite as long as the Hopi and are believed to have migrated from Canada and from even farther north. Their storytellers will explain that the mountains bordering their land were created by First Man and First Woman. With other Holy People, they made Night and Day, the Sun, the Moon and the Stars. One day they found a baby. They named her Changing Woman.

According to the legend, Changing Woman's twin sons—Monster Slayer and Born of Water—made the world safe for people by killing all of the dangerous beasts. Changing Woman eventually went away to live with the Sun. But before she went, she created the first Dine' clans.

Today, the Dine' live on the largest reservation in the United States—25,000 square miles that takes up most of northwestern

I'll Trade You

Trading posts were stores, clubhouses and newspapers all rolled into one and Navajos often traveled for hours on horseback or foot to get there. The trading post was their most important link to the outside world—sometimes their only one. They'd exchange the jewelry and rugs they made for all kinds of things they needed—everything from candy to coffee, pocketknives to calico. They'd get medicine if they were sick, meet their friends and get the news. Legal money rarely changed hands.

John Lorenzo Hubbell was the dean of the traders—and a friend to the Navajo. He nursed them through smallpox, taught them English and even helped settle family fights. Visit the Hubbell Trading Post on the Navajo Indian Reservation near Ganado,

(continued on page 26)

(continued)

Arizona, and you'll feel like you're back in those days a century ago when Hubbell was running the place. The baskets still hang from the ceiling and the counters are still stocked with goods. Navajo weavers are demonstrating their craft. Now a National Historic Site, it is one of the oldest trading posts on the Navajo Reservation. It's still a store, too, and just like in the old days, you can sell a rug or buy some candy. Now though, you better bring some money.

Arizona and stretches into New Mexico and Utah. They call their land Dine'tah. You could drive for miles and miles without passing a house—or a person. Some still herd sheep—the wool is used for their blankets and rugs. They also work as artisans or they farm, as they have for generations, though many Dine' today work in nearby cities and towns, too.

Tribal tradition is very important to Navajo families. The first time a Navajo baby laughs out loud, for example, is marked by a special celebration. They turn to medicine men to help cure sickness. Thousands gather every summer for the Navajo Nation Fair in Window Rock.

But even now no one has forgotten the especially sad time when the U.S. government forced them to leave their land in 1864 and take the "Long Walk" from Canyon de Chelly in Arizona to Fort Sumner, New Mexico, where they were kept in prison. Many people died along the way and in prison. Finally, four years later, they were set free and began to return to the land that had been set aside for them—just one tenth the size of what they'd left.

You'll still see the traditional eight-sided log and mud houses called *hogans* here built to always face the sunrise. Some Dine' families live at least part of the year deep in the rugged canyons of Canyon de Chelly. The sunrise is spectacular.

KIDS! TELL YOUR PARENTS:

The Hopis may not be particularly welcoming to outsiders. Especially at the Hopi Mesas, remember that you're visiting a neighborhood, not Disneyland. Visitors must check in at the Cultural Center immediately; calling ahead is best. Absolutely no wandering around without permission. You may not photograph villages or take anything from them. You and your parents may find there isn't much to see.

Your family will have to drive great distances to get to places you may want to visit. There's not a lot in between. Be forewarned that while the land is beautiful, there may be few things to see or do along the way. Take advantage of opportunities—and they're everywhere in Arizona—to learn about Native American culture. Hike around an ancient ruin.

In Phoenix, you can call the Heard Museum at 602-252-8840. In Flagstaff, call the Museum of Northern Arizona at 602-774-5213.

Check at the Hopi Cultural Center at 602-734-2401 (where a museum is located), or the Hopi Tribal Council Office at 602-734-2441 to see which villages are hosting visitors and if any upcoming dances will be open to the public. Frequently, there is not a lot of advance notice.

For more information about the Navajo Nation, call Navajoland Tourism at 602-871-6659. Call Petrified Forest National Park at 602-524-6228; Meteor Crater at 602-289-2362, and Lowell Observatory at 602-774-3358.

LAS VEGAS
THE PLACE THAT NEVER SLEEPS

Here's one place where you don't have to worry about being afraid of the dark. Las Vegas never turns out the lights. The doors to the hotel-casinos never close—even on Christmas. If your mom and dad would allow it, you could play the latest video games in gigantic hotel arcades all evening long. You've never seen so many different games in one place.

You've never seen so many huge lights either as you'll see walking down Las Vegas's famed Strip where so many hotels and  casinos are concentrated. In fact, you could power 3,300 houses in the middle of the desert on what it takes to keep the lights burning on the Strip and at the casinos around town.

Las Vegas, of course, is famous for legalized gambling. The action never stops—not even in the middle of the night. Kids aren't permitted to gamble—or even be in a casino. But there's never been more for kids to do here.

Las Vegas was built right in the desert. Nevada was the first state to legalize gambling and was known for gangsters like "Bugsy" Siegel who ran the hotels and for glitzy adult entertainment—from comedians to show girls to singers.

Sun Smarts

Be careful out there! The desert sun is very strong—even if it's not hot outside.

Sun burns really hurt. But you can avoid them easily.

- Smear on sunscreen whenever you go outside. Find one with a Sun Protection Factor (SPF) of at least 15. If you're going to be swimming, get a sunscreen that's water resistant.

- Take a break every 90 minutes or so and head into the shade.

- Get plenty to drink.

- Wear a tight-weaved cotton shirt (T-shirts won't help much) and a hat.

No one thought of Las Vegas—the name means "the meadows" in Spanish—as a town for kids or families. But that's all changed now. Three new hotels have been built with you in mind. Within a few blocks, you can go from ancient Egypt at the River Nile to Medieval England to a Caribbean Pirate Battle to the circus and to the Land of Oz.

FACT:

A couple gets married in Las Vegas every seven minutes — even in the middle of the night.

You'll find rides everywhere. Try the Canyon Blaster, the only double-corkscrew indoor roller coaster in the U.S. at Circus Circus's new Grand Slam Canyon, and then duck inside the hotel to catch some of the circus acts.

If you're visiting in the summer, head for Wet 'N Wild—the huge water park. Take the boat ride around the River Nile inside of the Luxor Hotel—it holds enough water to fill five Olympic-sized swimming pools. Or, search for the obelisk in a heart-stopping motion-simulator ride that takes you into an underground pyramid to battle a power-grabbing cult leader.

Watch the nightly pirate show in front of the Treasure Island Hotel.

FACT:

The new MGM Grand Hotel and Grand Adventures Theme Park, the world's largest hotel, employs more than 8,000 people. That"s enough people to fill up an entire town. If all 5,005 rooms are filled, there would be more people than in many towns in Iowa.

FACT:

The most powerful light beam in the world shines from the top of the pyramid-shaped Luxor Hotel, which opened in 1993. A person could read a newspaper by the light 10 miles into space.

Several times a night, a pirate ship battles a British frigate—complete with cannons and men overboard. Down the street, you can watch a volcano erupt in front of the Mirage or go inside and watch the dolphins perform tricks.

You can't miss the gigantic gold MGM lion outside the biggest place in town. The MGM Grand Hotel Casino is the largest hotel in the world with 5,005 rooms. And it comes with the MGM Grand Adventures amusement park, the city's first theme park. It is small compared to Disneyland, but you can have several hours of fun on the rides and shows. It has an indoor roller coaster, a water ride that takes you "Over the Edge" and lots of cartoon characters.

But Las Vegas isn't all glitz and action. It boasts one of the West's most famous "educational" attractions—Hoover Dam. About 30 miles outside the city, the 726-foot-high hydroelectric dam was built in the 1930s to control flooding. Today, it remains the largest arched-gravity dam ever built and supplies water for nearly 25 million people.

It also created Lake Mead, the world's largest artificial

reservoir. Millions of people head to Lake Mead National Recreation Area every year to boat or swim or just chill out.

Don't forget the desert either. Head to Red Rock Canyon to hike around huge pink, red and purple sandstone rock formations. You might even see a bighorn sheep or a coyote. Or drive 50 miles and you've found Valley of Fire. It's 56,000 acres full of all kinds of wind- and water-

FACT:

Hoover Dam provides enough power to supply half a million homes for a year.

Bryce and Zion

Millions of years of wind and water have etched out the giant pink cliffs of Bryce Canyon National Park in Utah with rock pinnacles that look like people. There's even a group of formations that look like a chess set. You can hike around—or drive along the rim—and see how many shapes you can find in the tall spires.

Not far away is Zion National Park with its towering cliffs. The Virgin River—which carved those cliffs—still flows along the floor. You'll see all kinds of rock formations here—cliffs, sheer rock walls and strange shapes. Early Indians believed the huge 2,600-foot-tall Watchman formation was a symbol of power. Don't miss the Watchman—a huge spire near the entrance.

sculpted sandstone that seem made to climb up, through and around—complete with spooky caves. It gets its name from the red and orange color of the rock. You won't find any glitz out here. Just lots of lizards.

KIDS! TELL YOUR PARENTS:

Las Vegas hotels are huge places teeming with people. It's easy for kids to get lost—even big ones. Make sure you keep a close watch on your parents, too!

And BEWARE OF ARCADE-MANIA! Older kids probably have never seen so many arcade and video games in one place. You won't ever want to quit. Your parents probably will set some time or dollar limits (most games cost at least a quarter).

Also remember that kids aren't permitted in the casinos. Don't assume you can watch your parents gamble or play slot machines. You can't. Casino officials will order you out as soon as they see you.

At least two hotels—the Las Vegas Hilton and the new MGM Grand—offer in-house child care and children's activities. The Hilton even allows kids to stay overnight in its "Youth Hotel."

You can call 800-NEVADA8 for tourist information.

Call Bryce Canyon at 801-834-5322 and Zion National Park at 801-772-3256.

JEROME, SEDONA, AND BISBEE
MINES AND GHOSTLY PLACES

There weren't many roads then so they came on horses and mules and burros—a rough and tumble group who all had the same goal: Get rich quick. Most left poor. They were the prospectors and miners who made their way up the mountain to Jerome and to other fast-growing towns in Arizona to dig gold, silver, copper and other minerals from the mines that were being dug deep underground.

When a mine was rich—like Jerome's famous copper deposits, Oatman's gold and Tombstone's silver—a town would spring up overnight—a whole city of tents and shacks. It wasn't very safe or comfortable. Jerome's tent city burnt to the ground twice in two years between 1897 and 1899.

After that, serious building began in Jerome, six miles up Mingus Mountain. The town is built hugging the mountain on top

FACT:

The number one gemstone produced today in Arizona is turquoise.

of 88 miles of mining tunnels. At its peak, in the 1920s, 15,000 people lived here—making it one of the largest cities in Arizona. But like other Arizona mining towns, when the mine died, so did the town. Jerome became a ghost town with fewer than 100 people.

Now it's come back to life, though it still seems kind of spooky with its old buildings and steep roads up and down the mountain.

FACT:

The Colorado River runs down most of the Arizona-California border before entering Mexico and emptying into the Gulf of California.

Many artists live and work here. You can learn about mining at the Jerome State Historic Park and at the Jerome Historical Society Mine Museum, where you can see all of the gear the miners used and learn about different rocks and minerals.

If you want to look for more ghosts, head one mile up the mountain from Jerome to the Gold King Mine and Ghost Town. This used to be a town called Haynes where they struck gold. Now it's a fun place to visit where you can see all kinds of old machinery, pet the burros or even, with a prospector's help, pan for gold (it's not as easy as you think). Don't miss the hermit's cave. A hermit still lives there!

There are ghost towns all over Arizona that you can visit. Some, like Oatman, Tombstone and Bisbee, have been fixed up again like they used to be. Others are just some crumbling buildings. There are bound to be plenty of ghosts everywhere.

For a different kind of mystery, head down the mountain from Jerome to Sedona. A lot of people believe there are sources of powerful electromagnetic energy here. They're called "vortices." The power comes, believers say, from natural energy seeping out of the earth. Psychic powers and emotions are stronger here — you'll see people reading tarot cards around town. Lots of artists live here, too.

Some say because of all of this energy, UFOs visit here. The Bell Rock Vortex is said to be a good spot to watch for UFOs. You

Bisbee

Strap on your miner's gear—from a waterproof slicker to a hard hat and battery-pack light and head down 800 feet at the Queen Mine in Bisbee for the largest underground mine tour in the country. Bisbee, in southeastern Arizona near the Mexican border, is a funky town where a lot of artists now live. Check out their work at different galleries around town.

But Bisbee's main claim to fame has always been its mines. From 1877 until the Queen Mine closed in 1944 over 8 billion pounds of copper were taken out. It was the richest copper mine of that era. So much mining was done around Bisbee that there are 2,500 miles of underground tunnels here. There's also the huge Lavender Pit that was dug to reach more copper ore.

Stop in at the Bisbee Mining and Historical Museum. It helps bring alive the people who lived in Bisbee then—the prospectors and bankers and boarding house proprietresses.

Down in the Queen Mine, you'll travel over the same track the miners used. Your guide—likely a former miner himself—will show you how they'd blast with dynamite sticks to get deeper into the rock. You'll see the tunnels that crisscross the mine.

Don't miss the "honey wagon"—the traveling port-a-potty-on-wheels that traveled down the track all through the mine. These were the only bathrooms the miners had. No privacy, though.

can hike around Boynton Canyon Vortex, picnic at Cathedral Rock Vortex and admire the view from Airport Mesa Vortex.

You can also search for your own special vortex nearby in Red

Rock Country, the huge weird-shaped sandstone mesas and canyons that surround Sedona. It's fun to hike or take a jeep tour out amid the Red Rocks. They really look red and seem to turn different colors as the light changes. You may recognize the landscape from westerns and commercials you've seen. Many are filmed here.

One special spot high in the rocks is an ancient cliff dwelling called Honaki where you can climb in and out of the crumbling

Ready, Set, Slide...

No chlorine here. At Slide Rock State Park—it's half-way between Sedona and Flagstaff—you're in a natural water park. Local kids think there's no better spot when it's hot. Hit the rocks in the middle of the pool that was carved by the waters of Oak Creek and you'll slide downstream. When you get tired of sliding, climb out onto the rocks to rest. There's plenty of hiking here, too.

And apples. The park originally was homesteaded by farmers who grew them here.

rooms the Indians built out of the rock. At one time, there were 200 rooms here.

Look for children's fingerprints in the mud mortar that holds the stone blocks together. When the walls were being built, guides will tell you, the kids all helped—even the little ones. It looks like they used their fingers to plug the gaps between the stone bricks with more mud. They must have had fun.

KIDS! TELL YOUR PARENTS:

Ghost towns are fun to explore, but be forewarned: some are considerably off the main track on bumpy roads. For more information on where to find ghost towns in Arizona—and what you'll find when you get there—call the Arizona Office of Tourism at 602-542-TOUR.

If you get to a ghost town, you can have fun talking about what life must have been like for the children who lived there.

To find out more about the vortices in Sedona, try the non-profit Center for the New Age at 602-282-1949. They've got free maps to the areas.

It's worth a detour to go on the Queen Mine Tour. Call 602-432-2071.

TUCSON AND ARIZONA
CACTUS, COWBOYS AND FLY BALLS

They're in almost every cowboy movie you've ever seen— the gigantic weird-shaped saguaro (pronounced "sa-wa-row") cactus with long spiny-skinned arms that point straight up. Cowboys still ride amid them—you can, too, if you visit Phoenix or Tucson.

But look closely and you'll see that saguaro cacti are a lot more than just big plants that live in the desert: they're condos

FACT:

Gila monsters are two feet long—the biggest native lizards in the continental U.S. They're also the deadliest—one of only two poisonous lizards in the entire world.

for animals. Like the Gila woodpecker or white-winged dove or screech owls who peck apartments inside the cactus. Inside, the animals are cozy and safe from the desert heat—and night cold.

People have used the saguaro for hundreds of years—making jelly from its fruit and fences from its wood-like ribs.

The saguaro cactus is the giant of the desert—some grow to be 50 feet tall and weigh 8 tons—as much as several cars put together. It takes them 150 years to get that big. Even after years of drought, the saguaro has enough moisture inside to produce its pretty white flowers—the state flower of Arizona.

You'll only find saguaro cactus in the Sonoran Desert in the Southwest. See them closeup by driving or hiking around the Saguaro Monument in Tucson—one part is on the west side of Tucson, the other across town on the east side. Watch out for the windy roads, though. They may

FACT:

Tiny hummingbirds —some aren't even three inches long— can race through the air at 30 miles per hour. They're also the only birds that can fly backwards.

Tubac

Most weekends through the fall and spring, at the tiny town of Tubac south of Tucson, kids and parents alike are busy digging up the story of early Spanish settlers.

Tubac, now a town full of artists and galleries, began as a mission outpost in 1730. A military base later was established here that blossomed into a big settlement—one of the most important in the Southwest.

Today, just a few hundred feet from the town, are more than 12 acres of ruins from as many as 200 buildings. It's called the Colonial Tubac Archeological Park. Volunteers have helped find all kinds of artifacts—coins, pieces of pottery and the foundations of the old buildings. It doesn't cost anything to dig. Kids over 13 can stay without their parents. Just call 602-820-5492. And don't forget to check out the galleries while you're here.

make you dizzy.

Head to the Arizona Sonoran Desert Museum nearby to learn a lot more about the saguaro and many other plants and animals that call the Sonoran Desert home. More than 200 animals and 1,200 plants live here in the zoo—everyone thinks it's one of the best in the country—in their natural desert environment—from Gila monsters to tarantulas to mountain lions, coyotes and snakes. This is also a place where injured animals are nursed back to health. Don't miss the aviary where all different kinds of hummingbirds buzz around, or the "living cave" complete with running underground stream. Colossal Cave, the world's largest dry cavern, is just outside Tucson.

FACT:

The kangaroo rat can survive without ever drinking water.

FACT:

A snake's skin feels like silk.

To see a different kind of bird in Tucson, head to the famous Pima Air Museum where you'll find one of the biggest collections of historic planes in the world—World War II

Shootout at the O.K. Corral

Before Ed Schieffelin set out from the fort, soldiers warned the prospector that all he'd find in the hills would be his tombstone—at the hands of angry Indians. So when he struck a mountain of silver, he gleefully called his town Tombstone. It became known as "the town too tough to die."

But Tombstone is remembered now not for the silver but for 30 seconds at the O.K. Corral—the most famous gunfight in the history of the Wild West.

The Earp brothers and the Clanton gang were known enemies. Wyatt Earp was a U.S. Marshal; the Clantons were outlaws. On the afternoon of October 26, 1881, they met at the O.K. Corral. The Earps' friend Doc Holliday was there too.

When it was over, three of the Clantons lay dying. Virgil and Morgan Earp were seriously wounded. The dead were buried at Boot Hill Graveyard.

Later, the Earps and Holliday were cleared of murder charges but the hatred continued. A few months later, Virgil Earp was shot, his arm crippled; his brother Morgan was killed soon after. Wyatt Earp left Tombstone for good—once he'd killed the men he believed had murdered his brother.

combat planes and helicopters among them.

Many people like to see the famous Mission San Xavier del Bac. Kids like to climb the hill behind it.

But everyone really comes to this part of the country to see cowboys. And you don't have to go far to find them, wearing cowboy boots and hats. There are dude ranches here where you

Geronimo

He was a Chiricahua Apache and lived in peace with his people—until Mexican troops killed his wife, children and his mother. Then Goyahkla vowed revenge. He fought the Mexicans with more ferocity than any other Apache Chief. The Mexicans called him Geronimo.

At about the same time, in the 1870s, Americans began to move into Apache territory. There were times of peace—but more times of fighting. Finally, the government decided all of the Apache must move from their homelands to a reservation. Geronimo, who wouldn't go, was captured and put in prison. He escaped. Over the years, he and his band of Apache would agree to return to the reservation, only to leave again. They felt the promises made to them weren't kept. Geronimo finally surrendered in 1886 in Arizona. He died at Fort Sill, Oklahoma, in 1909.

Years later, during World War II, American paratroopers jumping out of planes would remember his fight for his people's freedom. They'd yell "Geronimo."

can spend a week learning to ride (bring shoes with heels if you plan to ride, the wranglers will tell you). Then there's Old Tucson Studios just down the road from the zoo. Hundreds of movies, commercials and TV shows have been filmed here with famous stars such as Clint Eastwood and John Wayne. You might get a chance to watch a movie being made.

You'll certainly get to see a gunfight, watch an Old Western magic show or play in the special "Kids Korral." That's especially fun for little kids.

For more Wild West fun near Phoenix, kids like to head for Rawhide in Scottsdale. It's an entire Old West town complete with saloon, Western restaurants, stores, Cowboy entertainers and friendly burros.

At Pioneer Arizona Living History Museum, you can learn what life was like for pioneer families who settled here 100 years ago. Watch people dressed as pioneers work in the village as they would have then—shoeing horses or cooking on outdoor fires, for example. Check out the one-room schoolhouse.

Then for some modern family fun in the sun, there's Scottsdale. The sun shines most days of the year (it's really hot in the summer!) and there's never been more for kids and their parents to do here—swimming, playing tennis, riding. Several big resorts tout all their kids' activities.

Then there's baseball. Lots of families who can't wait for the season to start come here to watch spring training. The parks are small, so you'll get a good close-up of your favorite players from the Chicago Cubs, California Angels, Oakland A's, San Diego Padres, San Francisco Giants, Seattle Mariners, Milwaukee Brewers and Colorado Rockies at their practice fields in—what else?—the Cactus League. Don't forget your mitt.

KIDS! TELL YOUR PARENTS:

Winding roads can make even the strongest stomachs queasy—especially little ones. Eat lightly and look out the windows as you drive, not at a book or game in your lap. Ask your mom or dad to check with your doctor about some motion sickness medicine if you tend to get car sick.

If you're hankering to try a dude ranch, the Arizona Office of Tourism can provide a list. Call 602-542-8687. Tanque Verde Ranch in Tucson is well known for its children's programs (602-296-6275). Camp Hyatt started at the Hyatt Regency Resort at Gainey Ranch—and it's widely credited with leading the trend for kids' programs at hotels around the country. Camp Hyatt Kachina now runs every day of the year. Call Hyatt reservations at 800-233-1234.

The Phoenix & Valley of the Sun Convention & Visitors Bureau can provide the Cactus League schedule and ticket information. They'll have info about hotels and resorts running children's programs (602-254-6500).

Call Old Tucson Studios at 602-883-0100; Rawhide at 602-563-5600 and the Pioneer Arizona Living History Museum at 602-993-0212. The phone for the Arizona Sonoran Desert Museum is 602-883-2702 and for the Pima Air Museum call 602-574-9658.

WHITE SANDS NATIONAL MONUMENT
SAND SURFERS

You've never seen so much sand—miles and miles of the stuff, sweeping white dunes 60 feet high.

Slide down the dunes—with a sled or without (a heavy piece of cardboard works too!). Hike up and around them. The sand is packed pretty hard.

White Sands National Monument is fun no matter what you do. It's awesome to look at, too. Here, at the northern end of the Chihuahuan Desert near Alamogordo, New Mexico, is the largest gypsum sand dune field in the world—275 square miles. White Sands preserves a lot of it—along with plants and animals that can survive here.

White Sands Missile Range completely surrounds the park. It was first used to test rockets that were captured from the Germans during World War II. Today, rockets and weapons are

FACT:

Astronauts practice space shuttle landings at the White Sands Space Harbor. In an emergency, the shuttle could land here. That has only happened once. On March 30, 1982, the shuttle Columbia landed here because the ground was too soggy at Edwards Air Force Base in California.

still tested here on the 4,000-square mile range. That's why it's closed to the public (so is the park, for safety, when a test is in progress). You can learn more about rockets nearby at the Space Center in Alamogordo, where the capsule and spacesuit used by HAM, the

first chimpanzee in space, and a moon rock and rockets are displayed. During the summer, kids come from all over to attend "Shuttle Camp" and learn more about space.

At White Sands National Monument, you'll

see very special sand. It's gypsum, which is different from other rocks because it dissolves more easily in water, like salt. When rain falls on the mountains that form the Tularosa Basin surrounding White Sands, the layers of gypsum in the rock gradually dissolve and run down the mountains in the water. But at the bottom, there's nowhere for it to go. There are no rivers in the Tularosa Basin here.

The rainwater is trapped. It collects on the bottom of the basin—in Lake Lucero. The lake is a "playa," a dry lakebed that only has water after a heavy rain. It's here that the fantastic glistening dunes begin to form. As the water evaporates, the gypsum that's left begins to form beautiful crystals called selenite. These crystals break into tiny pieces that become sand.

FACT:

Gypsum is a mineral that is used to make "drywall" (sometimes called "sheetrock"), which is used to build the inside walls in most modern houses.

The blowing winds arrange the sand into dunes. They are constantly growing and changing! Slowly, the sand will cover everything in its path.

Indian legend has it that there's the ghost of a beautiful

Mexican maiden named Manuela who haunts the dunes. Her lover was a young Spanish explorer who was killed by Indians at

Smokey

Smokey the Bear was a symbol before he was real—a loveable bear made up as a way to teach kids and grownups about fire safety. He was first introduced 50 years ago—in 1944—and was a hit from the start. Every kid in America knows his slogan: "Only YOU can prevent forest fires."

Then, one day in 1950, fire fighters in Capitan, New Mexico, struggling to put out a huge forest fire, found the real Smokey. They discovered a tiny, frightened five-pound bear cub clinging to a blackened pine tree. He had been burned and they took him to an animal hospital. When he was well, Smokey went to live at the National Zoo in Washington, D.C. Thousands of children came to see him over the next 25 years. He's buried now in Smokey Bear State Park in Capitan, near where he was found. You can learn more about Smokey and fire safety there and see the old Smokey posters and toys kids liked. It's not far from Ruidoso.

Take care to always pour water over your campfires to make sure they're extinguished. Even a small breeze can cause a fire to spread. Trees can't run away from fire like you can.

the edge of the dune field. Manuela had left her home to search for him but was never seen again. The legend says she comes nightly in her flowing white wedding gown to the dunes where her lover was lost and buried.

You may not see her ghost but you will find four different kinds of dunes here:

- Dome, or "baby" dunes, are the first ones to form. They're low mounds of sand. (You might not see any because they're only found near the shores of Lake Lucero where the dunes start to form.)

- Transverse dunes are long ridges of sand and can be very tall.
- Barchan dunes are crescent shaped—like a new moon (the arms of these dunes always point in the direction the wind is blowing). They move as much as 12 feet per year.
- Parabolic dunes look like an inside-out barchan dune.

  Slide and climb as long as your parents let you. But be careful. Don't tunnel into the dunes. They collapse easily.

You can hike around the dunes on the Big Dune Nature Trail and look for different plants and animal tracks. It's hard to survive here but some animals, such as kangaroo rats, lizards and pocket mice, have adapted to living in the desert.

Almost all desert animals stay deep underground—where it's cooler—during the day and come out to look for food when the sun goes down.

But the landscape they find when they start exploring isn't all the same. In fact, there are four very different deserts in this part of the country. Part of the Great Basin Desert—it's also called the

Painted Desert—is northeast of Flagstaff. It's got lots of jagged canyons, mesas and tall rocks that are hundreds of feet high. The Mojave Desert, at Arizona's north-western edge, is the driest, getting just a few inches of rain each year. No other desert in the country is as hot.

The Sonoran is the most famous—more colorful, more varied, with hundreds of different birds and other animals. Lots of people live in the

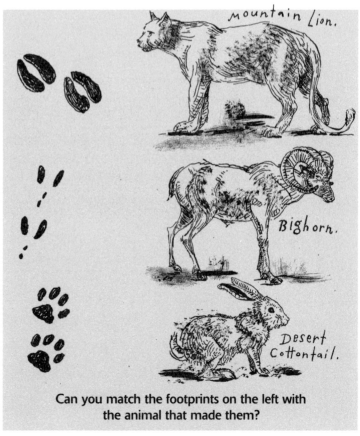

mountain Lion.

Bighorn.

Desert Cottontail.

Can you match the footprints on the left with the animal that made them?

Sonoran desert. You're in the middle of it in Tucson and Phoenix.

White Sands National Monument is at the northern end of the Chihuahuan Desert, which stretches from New Mexico and Texas into Mexico.

The ghost of Manuela has a lot of ground to cover.

KIDS! TELL YOUR PARENTS:

Remember that no matter when you visit, the desert sun is going to be hot. Smear on plenty of sunscreen, and on your parents too! Wear sunglasses. And drink plenty of fluids. At White Sands National Monument, you'll want to carry water and snacks with you: you'll be miles away from the visitors' center. If you're out late in the day, you'll want to have jackets handy. It gets cool fast when the sun goes down.

You should never hike alone. It's easy to get your direction confused.

For information about White Sands National Monument call 505-479-6124.

Elsewhere in the desert, rattlesnakes are common, but you likely won't see any. They don't come out in the heat of the day. But be careful if you're hiking. Never put your hands where you can't see and watch where you walk. You don't want to surprise any poisonous scorpions or black widow spiders either.

CARLSBAD CAVERNS
STALACTITES, STALAGMITES AND THOUSANDS OF BATS

They've got names like Whale's Mouth, Witches Finger and Lion's Tail.

That's exactly what they look like too. They're spooky and gigantic—and all made out of rock deep underground.

You don't know where to look first as you explore Carlsbad Caverns National Park. You can enter from the huge natural opening as the early cave explorers did. They faced pitch blackness and didn't know what to expect as they crawled and climbed into the darkness. Ancient Indians had been here before them— you can see the pictographs they left on the walls near the entrance. There were no trails then. The early explorer Jim White told such fantastic stories about what he'd seen that, at first, he had trouble getting people to believe him. After he convinced friends to explore with him, the stories spread and by the 1920s people began to come from all over to see the underground wonders. They still do. And cave explorers and scientists continue to uncover new portions of the cave.

For visitors like you, of course, there are paved walkways and plenty of light. There are actually more than 80 caves here at the National Park. But only 2 are open to the public. Carlsbad Caverns—with 30 miles of mapped trails—is the most famous. You've got your choice of 3 routes: Hike the one-mile natural entrance tour and you'll see the passage where the bats roost, Devil's Spring, Whale's Mouth and Devil's Den. From the natural entrance, you hike down *750* feet. Check out the Iceberg Rock, a 200,000 ton boulder that fell from the ceiling thousands of years ago.

FACT:

You could put 14 football fields inside the Big Room at Carlsbad Caverns. It's 1,800 feet long, 1,100 feet wide and 225 feet high—the largest room in a cave anywhere in the U.S.

But if you can't manage the hike—or your parents or little brother or sister can't—you can take an elevator down—in one minute you'll go down 750 feet. Then you can walk around the Big Room. Don't miss the 42-foot-high Twin Domes and the 62-foot-high Giant Dome in the Hall of Giants or the Bottomless Pit, a black hole 140 feet deep.

A ranger-guided tour of the King's Palace, Queen's Chamber,

Papoose Room and Green Lake Room is offered several times a day.

Some 20 miles from here at Slaughter Canyon, you can explore an undeveloped cave—no electricity or paved walks here—with a ranger (but you've got to reserve a spot ahead at the visitor center). Look for the amazing 89-foot-high monarch—one of the world's tallest underground columns—and the sparkling rock Christmas Tree.

FACT:

Deep within a cave, it's the same temperature all year round, a constant 56 degrees inside Carlsbad Caverns.

At Carlsbad Caverns, you'll see speleothems—the rock formations—everywhere. They look like frozen popcorn and soda straws and draperies, and that's what they're called. Some hollow soda straws grow to be several feet long—but never more than a half-inch thick.

How do you tell them apart? Stalactites hang from the ceiling (remember they hang "tite" to the ceiling) and stalagmites grow up from the ground (they "mite" reach the ceiling someday). They start with a drop of water that leaves a little ring of limestone on the ceiling. One after another, drops leave more

Bats

They spill out at night—hundreds of thousands of them whirling through the air—to gobble as many insects as they can find before they return at dawn. Every night in the spring and summer you can watch these Mexican free-tail bats as they leave Carlsbad Caverns in search of their dinner. (Check to see if the rangers are giving talks about them before they fly out.)

During the day, they crowd together on the ceiling of Bat Cave, a passageway near the natural entrance. This area is only open to scientists. The babies are born—as the mother bat hangs from her toes and thumbs from the ceiling. The baby hangs too and stays there for the next four weeks—even while the adults leave to search for food.

You can watch the bats fly out every night. Once a year, the park holds a "Bat Flight Breakfast" (usually on the second Thursday in August) and you can watch the bats return to the cave.

limestone. When the water flows fast enough, some drops to the floor and the limestone deposits grow up. Stalagmites are the biggest formations at Carlsbad Caverns. Giant Dome is the biggest—it's 62 feet high.

You'll see faces and animals and twinkling fairylands in the rock formations. The best part: no one will see in the cave exactly what you find.

There's plenty to do above ground too. The national park here includes a vast wilderness full of more than 700 different kinds of plants (look for the prickly pear cactus; you can eat the fruit!), more than 270 birds—cave swallows nest just inside the entrance of the cave in the warm months—and all kinds of other animals, snakes and lizards (look for them at night). And, of course, there are bats. You'll hear from the rangers about the tons of bat guano in the caves. Bat guano is kind of like cow pie. It makes good fertilizer.

FACT:

One bat can eat up to 900 insects per hour.

Another great place to look at animals from this region is at Living Desert State Zoological & Botanical State Park in the town of Carlsbad. All the animals are in their natural habitats so you get a chance to see what it's like where they live. One underground tunnel even lets you see animals that are active at night.

Look for the bobcats and prairie dogs, snakes and wolves, deer and foxes. Stare at them all you want. They may stare back.

KIDS! TELL YOUR PARENTS:

The cave paths can be slippery and steep. Make sure everyone is wearing good walking shoes. Rubber soles are best. Take along a light jacket or a sweater. The temperature is always 56 degrees in the cave. And stay on the trails. There are steep drop-offs just beyond and the fragile formations could be damaged by being touched.

You have to be old enough to make the hike from start to finish (unless your parents want to carry you). Strollers aren't permitted on the cavern paths.

Remember, if you want to explore Slaughter Canyon, you must make reservations ahead of time by calling the Carlsbad Caverns Visitor Center at 505-785-2232. These tours are not offered every day.

For more information about Carlsbad Caverns and the various guided tours and programs, call Carlsbad Caverns National Park at 505-785-2202. Call Living Desert State Zoological & Botanical State Park at 505-887-5516.

ALBUQUERQUE
CHILES, CONQUISTADORS, AND HOT AIR BALLOONS

The Spanish conquistadors came first in the mid-1500s. They were looking for the Seven Cities of Cibola that were so rich they were paved in gold. They never found them. They never really existed.

They did find the Indians who had been living here for centuries and decided they would try to convert them to their religion, Christianity. First, they settled in Santa Fe, 60 miles north of where Albuquerque is now. After a while, the Indians decided they'd had enough. They revolted in 1680. The Spanish fled.

Albuquerque officially became a town after the Spanish returned here, in 1706. Today you can walk around the Old Town where those early Spanish settlers lived and farmed. The adobe houses clustered around the Plaza (where you can buy souvenirs today) were once the early settlers' homes and businesses. (Don't miss the tiny American International Rattlesnake Museum, a conservation museum, where you can see 30 different varieties of

FACT:

Rattlesnakes make every effort to avoid contact with humans. Almost every bite is the result of someone trying to capture, kill or handle the snake.

FACT:

You can't steer a hot air balloon. You have to go up or down to where the wind is blowing in the direction you want to go. Most balloons are about 80 feet tall. They need 77,000 cubic feet of hot air to fly—enough to fill up a tall building.

Chile

New Mexicans put chile—they spell it with an "e" at the end, not an "i"—on everything, from scrambled eggs to chips, in sauces and stews.

They also hang "ristras"—the word means strings—of chiles everywhere. In the old days, the ristras were made and hung from rooftops to protect the drying red chiles from animals. Today, as was done then, the dried chiles are used to make chile powder and flakes.

Just as popular here are recipes with green chiles. They're picked before they're ripe and then roasted before they are used. Frequently, they're frozen to be used later. One's not necessarily hotter than the other—New Mexicans just explain the flavors are different. And they'll talk all night about which one—red or green—is better.

In fact, there are hundreds of hybrid varieties grown here, from mild to very hot. Kids grow up eating them. Keep some water nearby the first time you try some.

rattlesnake—including an albino.)

Today, tourists crowd Old Town—local kids say it's the best place in northern New Mexico to shop for souvenirs. In the old days, craftsmen lived here—weavers, carpenters and blacksmiths, among others. It was a major stop on the Camino Real, the trade route to Mexico. Later, the railroad came through and Albuquerque soon grew into a full- fledged city—it's now nearly 10 times bigger than any other town in New Mexico. Every

October, the Albuquerque International Balloon Fiesta is held here—the biggest in the world—where you can see 650 hot air balloons flying. Some are shaped like dinosaurs, witches, penguins and even Santa Claus.

Still today, Albuquerque is a mixture of the three cultures that were brought by those who settled here first—from the Indians in their pueblo to the Spanish explorers and missionaries to the Anglo traders who followed. You can learn more about the Pueblo Indians at the Indian Pueblo Cultural Center. In many parts of town, you'll hear Spanish spoken as much as English. And the food you'll eat here—from enchiladas (corn tortillas piled with cheese, beans and sometimes meat) to bizcochito cookies—reflect the way the cultures have blended together.

But long before the conquistadors arrived, prehistoric people lived here. Five dormant volcanos are on the outskirts of Albuquerque. Ancient hunters camped at the base of the lava flow, chipping some 15,000 pictures called petroglyphs into the rock. You can see them— snakes, circles and figures among them—at Petroglyph National Monument.

At the Albuquerque Museum, near Old Town, you can see the old armor that the conquistadors may have worn and learn more about the city's history. Check out the "History Hopscotch" exhibit downstairs that's especially for families.

So is the terrific New Mexico Museum of Natural History

FACT:

Millions of years ago, Sandia Crest— now a mountain peak more than 10,000 feet high—was covered by a great sea. Dinosaurs roamed the land that would become Albuquerque.

Turquoise Trail

They call it the Turquoise Trail but it's really just the back-roads way to travel the 60 miles from Albuquerque to Santa Fe. It's also got some fun stops along the way with plenty of kid-appeal.

Tinkertown is an entire Western town and circus that's built in miniature. There are thousands of figures here—drop in a coin and they come to life. There's the tiny old gold-mining town of Goshen and, 12 miles north, Madrid, which once was a booming coal mining town. Stop at the Mine Shaft Tavern for a hamburger. You can see mining and railroad cars at the Old Coal Mine Museum next door. (Don't forget to ring the train bell.)

across the street. Walk through a volcano. Watch huge dinosaurs fight and peer through glasses that let you see the way a dinosaur did. Head to the Naturalist Center where you can look through a microscope and make animal tracks in the sand.

Little kids will love the small Albuquerque Children's Museum nearby. No matter what your age, you'll like the Rio Grande Zoological Park, home to more than 1,000 animals. You can see more animals at the Rio Grande Nature Center—a 270-acre preserve along the banks of the Rio Grande—lizards, birds, and beavers included.

This is a town for all kinds of outdoor fun. In the winter, you can ski at Sandia Peak. You can take the Sandia Peak Tramway—the world's longest—up 2.7 miles to the summit all year round. In the spring and summer, you can watch the Albuquerque Dukes Play (they're the AAA farm team for the LA Dodgers) or head for Cliff's Amusement Park. Just pick your sport and get going!

KIDS! TELL YOUR PARENTS:

This might be a fun place to try some new foods. You'll have plenty of selection. But don't order anything too spicy at first. If you want to try chiles, order them on the side. You can use the chile-laced sauce as a dip for chips or tortillas. Have plenty of water handy.

The Albuquerque Convention and Visitors Bureau is the best place to start if you're looking for information about the city. Ask about the "30 Ways for Kids to Spell Fun in Albuquerque" brochure at 800-284-2282.

NEW MEXICO PUEBLOS
STORIES, DANCES AND POTS

They may be eagles or buffalo or, at Christmas, reindeer. Sometimes the boys—even little ones—and men paint their chests blue for the occasion. Other times they'll be brown. They could wear furry, scary-looking headdresses with horns or eagle feathers. Others might have fur hanging from the back of their belts like a tail, or leaves strapped to their arms. The girls balance tall headdresses. They wear lots of necklaces and bells.

Back and forth, they'll move in perfect time—sometimes hundreds at once—all to the beat of Indian drums. Kids who live at New Mexico's 19 pueblos begin learning these dances when they're little, and throughout their lives, they perform them. Watching them, you'll feel as if you've stepped onto a big movie screen.

They dance at feasts scheduled throughout the year at their pueblos for all sorts of reasons—the same way you might pray—for good health or to celebrate a good crop or for rain. Sometimes big crowds come to watch. But it's serious business because these dances are the way the Native Americans here express their love for nature and their religion.

The Indian Pueblo Cultural Center in Albuquerque is another great place to watch pueblo dancers. They perform every

Pueblo Etiquette

When you visit a Pueblo, you're visiting someone's neighborhood—not Disneyland or an outdoor museum.

- Be respectful of people's privacy. Don't wander into closed doors, up ladders or into streams that could be their only source of fresh water.

- Don't climb walls. They are very old and can be easily damaged.

- Don't try to enter the kiva, the ceremonial underground rooms. Non-Pueblo-members are not permitted there.

- Don't take anything—not even a piece of broken pottery.

- Ask before you take pictures. Sometimes you must pay for the privilege.

- At a Pueblo dance, act as you would in church or synagogue.
  Be quiet and don't talk to the dancers or to your friends. Remember, you're watching a religious ceremony. Don't applaud and don't take pictures.

weekend. Artists also show you how they weave, make pottery and jewelry.

Check out the Pueblo House Children's Museum while you're there. You'll see the traditional round oven called a *horno*. Pueblo families may have one outside their homes where they bake bread for special times. You can grind corn with a stone called a *mano* in a hollowed-out stone bowl called a *metate*—as they do. You can weave a mat, make a pictograph—the kind of drawing the ancient Indians painted in their homes

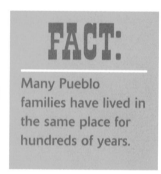

FACT:

Many Pueblo families have lived in the same place for hundreds of years.

alongside high cliffs—or try on ceremonial dress. It's lots of fun. You can try Indian fry bread—it's kind of puffy and chewy—at the Cultural Center restaurant.

The Native Americans here have lived in their pueblo villages for hundreds of years, following the traditions that have been handed down from older people to the children. There was a time many years ago when Spanish settlers thought the Pueblo Indians should be more like them. They outlawed their dances and tried to destroy their traditions.

Finally, the people in the pueblos had enough and attacked the settlers. Still today, Native Americans talk about the Pueblo Revolt of 1680, when their ancestors wouldn't give up their traditional ways.

Many of the buildings at the pueblos date from even before that time. They are made out of light brown adobe bricks. At the Taos Pueblo, you'll see the largest multi-storied pueblo building in the entire country. It's all made out of adobe—a mixture of mud and straw that's dried in the sun. There are ladders outside to get from floor to floor—no steps inside.

FACT:

Many Pueblo Indians celebrate Christmas by dancing.

While many pueblo families live nearby in modern homes like yours, some have lived here generation after generation in the flat-roofed adobe buildings that look like boxes stacked on top of each other. At some pueblos, like Taos, there is no electricity or running water so kids can't watch TV or take showers. They get water from a stream that runs through the pueblo. That's why if you visit, they

Heading for the Cliffs

Put on your sturdiest high-tops and head for the cliffs to see how children lived here more than a thousand years ago. They were Anasazi Indians, the ancestors of those who live in pueblos today.

One fun place to start is Bandelier National Monument, 46 miles west of Santa Fe. It's a great place to hike, picnic and look for animals—there are nearly 50 square miles of trails. Many people like to camp here too. Cliff ruins run along the northern wall of Frijoles Canyon for two miles. You'll see cave rooms that were carved out of solid cliff, the walls still black from the smoke of those families' fires, and walls that

(continued on page 82)

(continued)

were shaped out of blocks of rock. The most fun is climbing the four steep ladders—140 feet up—to the ancient Ceremonial Cave.

Imagine being a kid then and scampering up and down the cliffs all of the time. During the summer, the rangers can take you on special walks during the day and tell you Indian stories around campfires at night.

Nearby is the Puye Cliff Dwellings on the Santa Clara Pueblo land. There are ruins of hundreds of rooms, including huge underground kivas built near a mesa that's 7,000 feet at the top. You can climb up and down steep ladders to explore them. Look for the petroglyphs—drawings of animals, human figures and other symbols that were carved into the rock. Many are up high because the Indians stood on the rooftops to draw them.

don't like you to splash in the water. You can see more of their land—and learn more about their culture—by taking a horseback ride at the Taos Indian Horse Ranch nearby.

The different pueblo villages may look similar, but they have different languages, traditions and crafts. Different pueblos are known for different things.

The Zuni Pueblo, for example, is famous for carved animal fetishes that you'll see everywhere on necklaces. They are mostly made of stone or wood. People believe there is power in the spirit who lives in the fetish and that it can help you accomplish whatever you need to do. For example, the horny toad will bring you luck; the wolf will help you do it quickly and the bear will help keep you healthy.

Other pueblos are known for distinctive pottery and other crafts. You'll see smooth black pots from the Santa Clara Pueblo and painted ones from Acoma, drums from the Cochiti Pueblo, beadwork from Taos. You'll see beautiful silver jewelry everywhere and kachinas, the small carved dolls that represent everything from animals to plants.

FACT:

Pueblo people speak English in addition to their native language.

Storytelling is one important tradition everywhere. During the long winter months in the old days, young children would gather to hear a tribe elder tell ancient stories. Clay storyteller figures of a mother with children now are made by pueblo potters to commemorate the tradition.

And still today—in between homework and television and sports—kids are hearing those same ancient stories. They love them just as much.

KIDS! TELL YOUR PARENTS:

Be careful exploring the ancient ruins! They are irreplaceable and can be damaged by over-eager kids. Stay on the trails. Carry water and snacks. Remember, the ladders at Bandelier are steep. Your parents may want to keep your younger brothers or sisters at the bottom. There are no handrails at Puye and plenty of slippery rocks.

For more information about junior ranger programs at Bandelier call 505-672-3861. Call the Santa Clara Pueblo Tourism Office for information about Puye 505-753-7326, ext. 206.

If you're planning to visit a Pueblo, try to go when you can watch a dance. It's an experience you won't forget. The Indian Pueblo Cultural Center can provide an annual calendar of the Pueblo dances and its own schedule of special events; call 505-843-7270. Another source of information is the Indian Tourism Program at the New Mexico Department of Tourism, 505-827-7400.

SANTA FE AND TAOS
FIESTAS, MUSEUMS AND ART

You'll notice Santa Fe's buildings first. They look a lot different from the buildings in most towns—small and mostly brown, made out of mud-and-straw adobe bricks

FACT:

Chile is New Mexico's official state vegetable—even though it's a fruit. New Mexico grows more chile than anywhere in the country—53,000 tons a year. It's worth more than $456 million. The New Mexicans say they eat more chile than anyone in the country—even Texans.

that were hardened in the sun. Many are very old, set on narrow twisting streets.

That's because Santa Fe was a town 10 years before the Pilgrims even left England. In fact, you can walk around the oldest public building in the entire country—the Palace of Governors—in Santa Fe's Plaza, the heart of the town. It's a museum now where you'll find all kinds of things from the early days—old muskets, a chuck wagon, clothes and maps. Outside, stop and talk to the many Native American artists you'll see sitting on blankets, displaying the jewelry they want to sell. Tell them which necklaces you like.

Wherever you are in Santa Fe, you'll see a mixture of the different cultures—Spanish, Mexican, Indian and Anglo people have all lived here together for generations. You'll see all their different heritages come together in everything from the art to the food to the festivals.

Santa Fe's biggest party—the Fiesta de Santa Fe—celebrates these different cultures and is held every September. It's the oldest community celebration in the country and has been around since 1712—64 years before the Declaration of Independence. If you're visiting during the Fiesta, you can march in the Pet Parade with Santa Fe kids and their pets. Some kids dress up as animals, too.

Christmas is another special time. The streets and rooftops are lined with *farolitos*, small paper sacks in which a lit candle is placed in sand. It's very pretty. (You'll see similar displays in Taos and Albuquerque too.)

FACT:

Santa Fe is over one mile above sea level.

No matter what season, Santa Fe is a town known for its museums, its music—the opera is world famous—its artists and its stores and food. Grown-ups and kids like to come here to eat and shop. One favorite among local kids is Tomasita's in an old railroad station (try the sopaipillas—puffy fried bread with honey). There are dozens of stores selling everything from cowboy boots to T-shirts with red chile peppers on them to Indian dolls. One favorite is Jackalope (named after a mythical animal cross-bred of a jackrabbit and an antelope). It's a huge store with every kind of Southwest treasure you could possibly want—pots and necklaces and Indian blankets. Most will be within your budget, too.

Chimayo

Thousands come here to this tiny town in the mountains every year for the dirt. It's very special dirt at the El Santuario de Chimayo that is said to have magic healing powers. Back in the early 1800s, the story goes, a man saw a shining light coming from under the ground. He dug up a crucifix, which was placed on the altar at a nearby church. The next day, the crucifix was found buried in its original spot. This happened again and again. Finally, a church was built where the crucifix was found and, ever since, people have come here for the healing power of the dirt. Thousands come during the annual Holy Week pilgrimage. You'll see discarded crutches and braces in the church's side rooms.

Chimayo is also famous for its weaving traditions. The Ortegas and the Trujillos have been weaving here for generations, each learning with tiny looms from their parents and grandparents. Today, children still learn the craft. You can visit their shops and others, where you can watch the skilled weavers working on large looms, weaving patterns into what will become colorful rugs and blankets, jackets and vests. You'll see that each design is different—just as is a painter's canvas.

More expensive treasures can be found at the more than 200 galleries here—many concentrated along Canyon Road. You'll see beautiful sculptures and paintings, old Indian necklaces and pottery. Be careful if you visit; many pieces are very delicate. The Shidoni Bronze Gallery is fun to visit. It's just north of Santa Fe

Los Alamos

At first, the place was a remote ranch school for sickly boys. In 1943, the Manhattan Project changed all that. Scientists gathered at Los Alamos in this remote mountain town for a top secret mission: To build an atomic bomb that would end World War II.

J. Robert Oppenheimer, a physics professor from California, steered the work of 30 brilliant scientists who had come from all over the country. There were hundreds—families of the scientists, technicians and clerks. At the end of a winding, dirt road, the newcomers found a temporary town that had been hurriedly built. Secrecy was the way of life: lab members couldn't even talk to relatives elsewhere or travel further than 100 miles.

They achieved their mission in 27 months: the first atomic bomb was detonated on July 16, 1945, at the Trinity Site in the New Mexico desert north of Alamogordo.

Three weeks later, on August 6, 1945, the world's second man-made bomb exploded over Hiroshima, Japan. On August 9 the third bomb devastated the city of Nagasaki. Both bombs killed thousands and left many others horribly injured. Japan surrendered five days later. "Fat Man" and "Little Boy," as the bombs were called, ended the war—but at great cost. Thus began the atomic age and the nuclear arms race.

Today, Los Alamos National Laboratory is known as one of the country's leading research centers, where thousands of scientists work.

You can get a better understanding of what they do—and of the history of the Manhattan Project—at the Bradbury Science Museum here. Check the schedules for the hands-on programs designed to teach kids about science.

and you can see lots of huge bronze sculptures in the garden outside. On weekends, you might be able to watch the sculpture being cast: they pour molten bronze into a huge mold. Next door, if you're lucky, you'll see glassblowers at work at the Tesuque Glassworks.

You can have your pick of museums. Near the Plaza, see beautiful paintings at the Museum of Fine Art, including many by one of New Mexico's most famous artists, Georgia O'Keeffe. Little kids love Santa Fe's Children's Museum. Another favorite is the Museum of International Folk Art, where you'll find thousands of toys and dolls and masks from around the world—the biggest collection anywhere. Many of the figures are shown in miniature replicas of villages—an Indian Pueblo, a Mexican Village, an African-American settlement in Louisiana, a circus. You could look at them all day without getting bored.

FACT:

The Santa Fe Trail was the first major Western trade route, first traveled by traders and merchants more than 20 years before the more famous Oregon and California Trails opened most of the West. Each spring wagons gathered in Missouri for the 900-mile trip to Santa Fe and trail's end.

The museum has many weekend workshops for families and children where you can make your own folk art.

Next door, at the Museum of Indian Arts, head to the Resource Center to try out a loom or play a drum or grind corn. You'll see all kinds of Native American art here—ancient pots and jewelry, and modern crafts.

Then head down a dirt path to the Wheelwright Museum. Look at the building carefully: it's shaped like a Navajo hogan, the traditional home. Modern Native American art is shown here. You'll have fun downstairs in the Case Trading Post. It's just like the real Navajo trading posts that were so important a century ago. You can buy colored corn necklaces, beaded pins or Indian dolls, among other things. On summer evenings, you can hear a Native American storyteller. Every fall, the Wheelwright holds a children's powwow.

You can learn more about Native Americans at the Museum of Indian Arts and Culture. Then, just outside of town, you can explore more about the Spanish heritage by going back in time

The Painter and the Indian Scout

When he was 15, Kit Carson ran away from home in Missouri and joined a wagon train heading to New Mexico. He became a skilled trapper, a respected Indian scout and translator who was fluent in several languages as well as many Indian dialects. He won fame and popularity nationwide for his key role as a guide and explorer who opened the West.

Carson is also remembered for his role in helping to end the Navajo Wars by persuading the Navajos that they should stop fighting. Carson was much respected by the Native Americans because he was a fearless fighter.

Though he traveled much, Carson lived much of his life in Taos at the hacienda he

(continued on page 94)

(continued)

bought for his bride Josefa Jaramillo in 1843. They raised eight children there along with some Native American children they took in. You can walk through Carson's home today, seeing how a frontier family lived. Some of his military uniforms are here, along with his guns, his wife's dresses and children's bed. Carson and his wife are buried nearby.

Georgia O'Keeffe arrived in Taos some 60 years after Carson died to spend the summer painting. Already an established artist, she was captivated by Taos's light and all that she saw there. Eventually, she moved to a remote ranch in Abiquiu, about 60 miles from Taos, where she lived and painted until her death in 1986—at age 98. She is celebrated around the world—one of the greatest American painters of this century—for her paintings of flowers, the red, white and black landscapes of New Mexico's mountains, and bleached skulls.

to see what life was like at a Spanish hacienda at El Rancho de las Golondrinas.

Santa Fe is also a good place for outdoor fun—hiking, biking, horseback riding and, in the winter, skiing.

So is Taos, about 70 miles north of here. You can take the high road to Taos for a scenic tour. Taos is tiny compared to Santa Fe and a very friendly place. Many families come to Taos to fish and to raft on the Rio Grande River as well as to ski. Check out the Rio Grande Gorge—with one of the biggest expansion bridges in the country.

Taos is also famous for its artists—and colorful history. Explorer and famous Indian scout Kit Carson lived here. So did artist Georgia O'Keeffe. Today all kinds of artists live here— writers and painters, sculptors and woodcarvers. You'll see their work displayed at galleries. You may see some of them working there.

Many people come here to see the Taos Pueblo, which is nearly 1,000 years old. On Pueblo land, you can learn more about Native American culture by riding at the Taos Indian Horse Ranch. Watch Indian drums being made from hollowed-out logs at Taos Drums, just south of town.

Or head to the Millicent Rogers Museum to see one of the best collections in the country of Indian jewelry and art as well as many Hispanic pieces. Stop at the Martinez Hacienda to see what it was like to live here when the only supplies came by oxcart over the mountains. People sought safety here from Indian raids. Don't forget to stop at the Taos Plaza. Even if you're there at night, you'll see the American Flag flying. That's because during the Civil War, Taos was taken over by the Confederates for a brief time. Kit Carson led the small band who raised the Union Flag over the plaza and guarded it night and day. Think about that when you pick out a T-shirt here.

KIDS! TELL YOUR PARENTS:

Many galleries, especially in Santa Fe, don't especially welcome children. Think hard before you visit. Are you old enough to look, but not touch? Can you understand you're looking at things that took someone a long time to produce, not a cheap souvenir? You might ask a gallery owner if he minds if you come inside. Tell your parents to ask locally for a gallery where children are welcome and where you might see artists working.

For more information about Santa Fe, a good place to start is Santa Fe Convention and Visitors Bureau, 800-777-CITY. Call the Taos County Chamber of Commerce at 800-732-TAOS. Ask about their new "Kids Guide to Taos." For New Mexico ski information, call 800-4NMSTAY.